Mary Charrington

Open Up

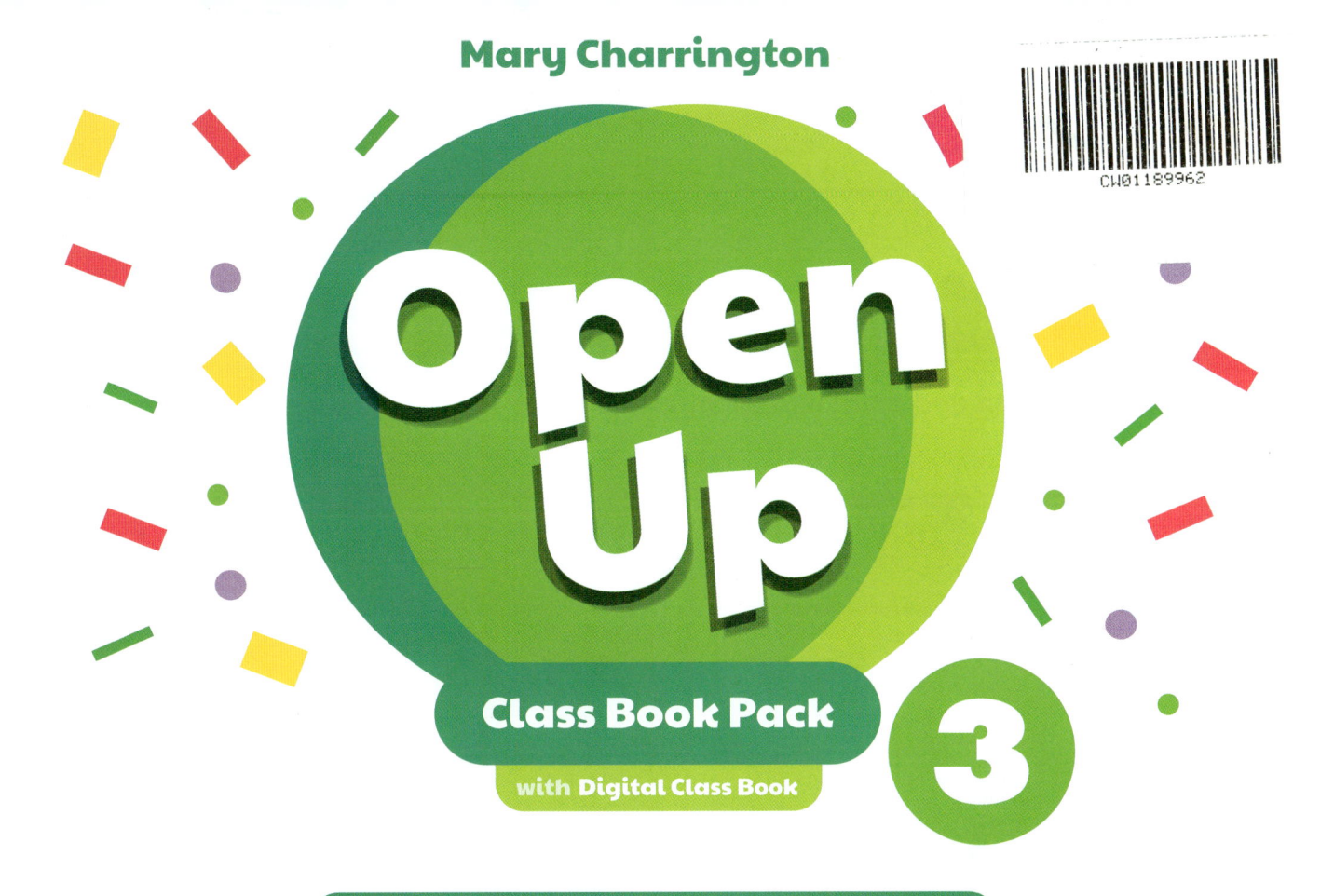

Class Book Pack
with Digital Class Book

3

OXFORD BLENDED SOLUTION
Use this code to access:

YOUR DIGITAL CLASS BOOK
- Fully interactive
- With audio and video
- Progress tracking

Go to oup.es/digital and enter your code

WYKJY47

Key Competences

	Cultural awareness and expression		Mathematical, Science, Technology and Engineering (STEM)		Citizenship		Entrepreneurship
	Linguistic communication		Personal, social and learning to learn		Digital		

OXFORD
UNIVERSITY PRESS

Lesson 1 Vocabulary

Starter Open Up

🎥 **Video**   1 🔊 001 Move, dance and sing.

2 🔊 002 Listen, read and point. Listen and repeat. Ask and answer.

Hi, my name's Leo. I'm 9. What's your name? How old are you?

Hello, I'm Mia. My favourite animal is a rabbit. What's your favourite animal?

1 Animals 71 👍
2 Bedroom 73 👍
3 Dressing up 65 👍
4 Fun 88 👍

3 🔊 003 Listen, point and repeat.   4 🔊 004 Listen and chant.

👍 10   👍 20   👍 30   👍 40   👍 50   👍 60   👍 70   👍 80   👍 90   👍 100

5 🔊 005 Listen and point. Say the number of 👍.

Numbers 20–100   Personal information

Lesson 2 Feelings — Starter

Wellbeing

1 🔊 006 Listen, point and repeat.

2 🔊 007 Listen and say the number.

1. energetic
2. bored
3. upset
4. strong
5. shy
6. brave

3 🔊 008 Listen, read and sing. Choose a feeling and sing again.

*How are you feeling? How are you feeling?
How are you feeling today?
How are you feeling? How are you feeling?
Open up and say.*

*Are you feeling energetic?
Or bored or upset?
Are you feeling strong?
Or shy or brave?*

*I'm feeling …
Open up to me.
How are you feeling?
You can tell me.*

4 Ask and answer. Open up and say.

— How are you feeling today?
— I'm feeling shy.

I'm Dan. I've got one brother and two sisters. Have you got any brothers and sisters?

6 Find, point and say more numbers.

— I can see number 39. It's on the bin.
— I can see number 51. It's on the poster.

bored brave energetic shy strong upset

3

Lesson 1 Vocabulary

1 Animals

Video 1 Remember the animals.

2 🎵 🔊 009 Listen, point and repeat. Say the number and the animal.

3 🔊 010 Listen for the sounds. Listen and chant.

| Pronunciation | scorpion /ɔː/ | frog /ɒ/ |

1 scorpion 5 parrot
2 dolphin   6 lizard
3 snake   7 butterfly
4 frog   8 worm

4 🔊 011 Listen, look and answer.

5 🔊 012 Listen and repeat. Play *What is it?* Describe and guess.

It's green. It's got four legs.

It's a frog.

Connect

What's your favourite animal?

Review It's got …   It hasn't got …

4

Lesson 2 Grammar **Unit 1**

Video

1 🔊 013 Listen and read. 💡 Act it out.

1. Wow! It's noisy.
2. It isn't noisy now. It's quiet.

Look at the babies. They aren't quiet. They're noisy. Listen!

2 🔊 014 Listen, read and follow. Listen and repeat.

+		-	
It's	noisy.	It isn't	quiet.
They're		They aren't	

3 🔊 015 Listen and chant.

Look!
It's = It is
It isn't = It is not
They're = They are
They aren't = They are not

4 🔊 016 **Mediation** Listen and say the number. Describe and guess in pairs.

It's big.
It's orange.

The lizard.

They're small.
They aren't noisy.

The worms.

5

Lesson 3 Song

Video 1 🔊 018 Dance and move. Think about the song. Say.

I feel …   shy   tired   excited   bored

2 🔊 019 Listen, read and sing. Describe the animals in the song and in the picture.

The animals song

Animals big, animals small
Animals long, animals tall
It's a wonderful world out there.
There are animals everywhere.

What's this, under this tree
Right here – next to me?
It isn't big, but it's long.
It's a snake. It's very long!

What's this, in this tree
Right here – up above me?
It's a parrot. It's noisy.
There are TWO. They're VERY noisy!

3 👥 Write new song lines. Change the words. ✏️

Our song
It's a … It's very …
There are two. They're very …

4 💡 Create actions for your song. **Talk bank** ⬇
Perform for your friends.

Let's clap our hands!   That's good.

Take part

Enjoy your performance.

6

Lesson 4 Culture | **Unit 1**

Animals that help us

▶ **Video** **1** Are these animals in the video? Say *Yes* or *No*.

birds   dogs   scorpions   dolphins

2 Look and say what you see.

3 🔊 021 Listen, read and point to the photos. How do dolphins help people in Laguna? Say.

Hi. I'm Ana. In Laguna, in Brazil, people and dolphins work together.

1 Look at this amazing bottlenose dolphin. It's got a long nose and it can jump high. Bottlenose dolphins are very intelligent and, guess what? They can help people.

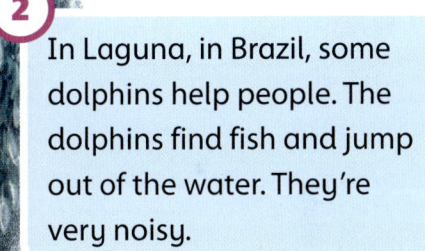

2 In Laguna, in Brazil, some dolphins help people. The dolphins find fish and jump out of the water. They're very noisy.

3 The fishermen put their nets near the dolphins. They catch lots of fish. The dolphins eat the fish, too. The dolphins and the fishermen are happy. They help each other. Wow!

fishing boat   net

4 Read and say *True* or *False*. Correct the false sentences. ✏️

1 Dolphins aren't intelligent.
2 Dolphins find fish for people in Laguna.
3 The dolphins aren't noisy.
4 The fishermen are sad.

5 👥 Make a list of animals that help us. ✏️

Dogs help people.

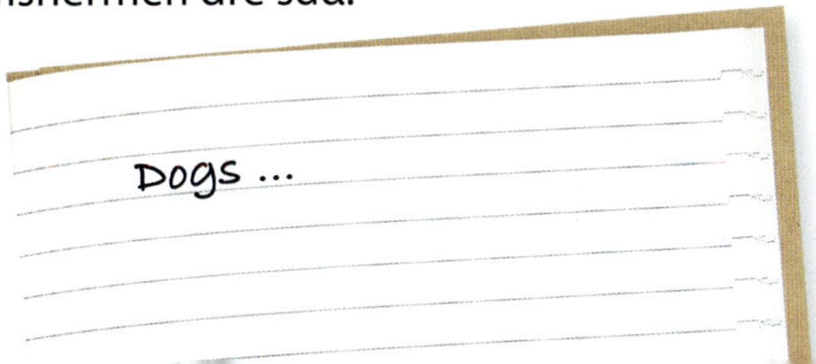

Dogs …

7

Lost in the forest

Video

1 🔊 023 **Listen, point and repeat.**

1 friendly   2 scary   3 dangerous   4 slimy   5 colourful

2 🔊 024 **Listen and read. What animals are in the forest?**

1 Carlos and Lucia are going on a nature walk.
- I want to see some cool animals!
- Have fun kids!

2
- What are they?
- Wow! They're fireflies.
- Are they dangerous?
- No, they aren't! They're cool!

3
- Hey, look! There's a snake!
- It's not a snake, silly! It's a worm.

4
- Is it slimy? Yuk!
- Yes, it is. It's cool, too! It's good for the earth.

5
- Hey, look. Snakes!
- Are THEY dangerous?
- Yes, they are!

6
- Carlos, look! There's a parrot.
- Is it friendly?
- Hello.
- Yes, it is. Hello, parrot.

8

Lesson 5 Story & Vocabulary   **Unit 1**

7 It's colourful, too. It's red, blue, green and yellow!

Let's follow it.

8 Where's the parrot? Where's the path?

I don't know.

I don't like the forest now. It's scary.

9 Don't worry. I can see the fireflies. There's home!

Wow! Thank you fireflies!

10 Hi kids! How's the forest?

It's amazing. There are lots of cool things in the forest!

3 Read, match and say.

1 It's colourful.

2 It's slimy.

3 It's dark and scary.

4 They're dangerous. They aren't friendly.

a   b   c   d

4 What does Carlos think about the forest? Share ideas and say.

It's boring.   It's dangerous.   It's scary.   It's cool.

Take notice

What do you notice about nature?

Review hat run spider window

9

Lesson 6 Story & Grammar

▶ Video   1 Story challenge   Answer the questions.

2 🔊 025 Listen, look and say the letter.

a Yes, it is.
b No, it isn't.
c Yes, they are.
d No, they aren't.

3 🔊 026 Listen, read and follow. Listen and repeat.

	?	+	-
Is it …	scary? friendly? dangerous?	Yes, it is.	No, it isn't.
Are they …	colourful? slimy?	Yes, they are.	No, they aren't.

4 Ask and answer about the animals in Activity 2.

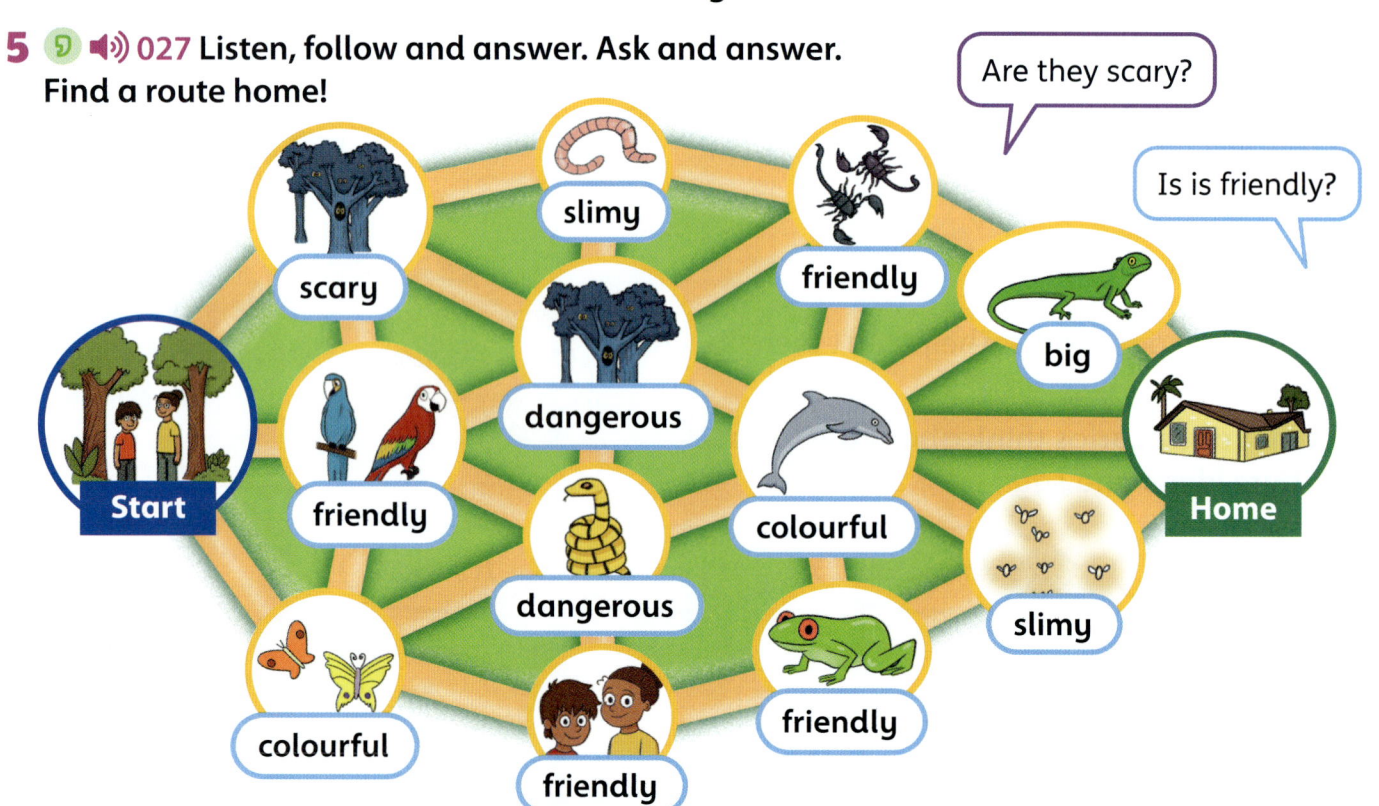

5 🔊 027 Listen, follow and answer. Ask and answer. Find a route home!

Are they scary?

Is is friendly?

Start — scary, slimy, friendly, dangerous, friendly, dangerous, colourful, friendly, big, slimy, friendly, colourful — Home

10

Listen and speak

Lesson 7 Skills   Unit 1

1 👁 Look and say what you see.   **2** 🔊 029 Listen and say the number.

① ② ③ ④

3 🔊 030 Listen and read. Listen and repeat. Act out the dialogue.

— Are you afraid of dogs?
— Yes, I am. Big dogs! Are you afraid of dogs?
— No, I'm not, but I'm afraid of spiders.

4 Speak up! Play the communication game. ✂ Cut-outs AB page 99

— Are you afraid of lizards?
— Yes, I am.

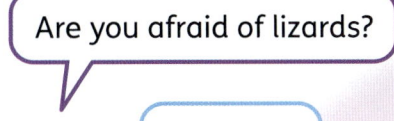

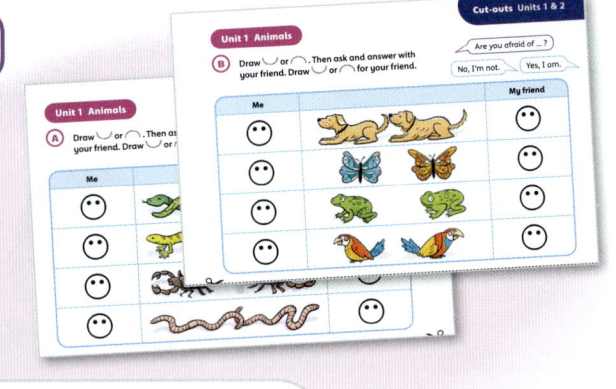

Care
Be kind when someone is afraid.

Are you afraid of … ?   Yes, I am.   No, I'm not.

11

Lesson 8 Review

Video

1. Play *Three in a row* with your class.

① Say 5 sentences.
- I'm afraid of …
- I'm not afraid of …

② Describe a scorpion!
- It's …
- It isn't …

③ Ask and answer about 3 dangerous animals.
- Is it … ?
- Yes, it is.
- No, it isn't.

④ Ask and answer about the butterflies.
- noisy?
- scary?
- colourful?
- slimy?

⑤ Answer the secret question.

?

⑥ Ask and answer about 3 small animals.
- Is it … ?
- Yes, it is.
- No, it isn't.

⑦ Say 2 animals for each adjective:
- friendly
- dangerous
- colourful
- scary

⑧ Describe the frogs.
- They are …
- They aren't …

⑨ Ask and answer about the parrots.
- Are they … ?
- Yes, they are.

2. Make up a secret question. Play the game with your friends.

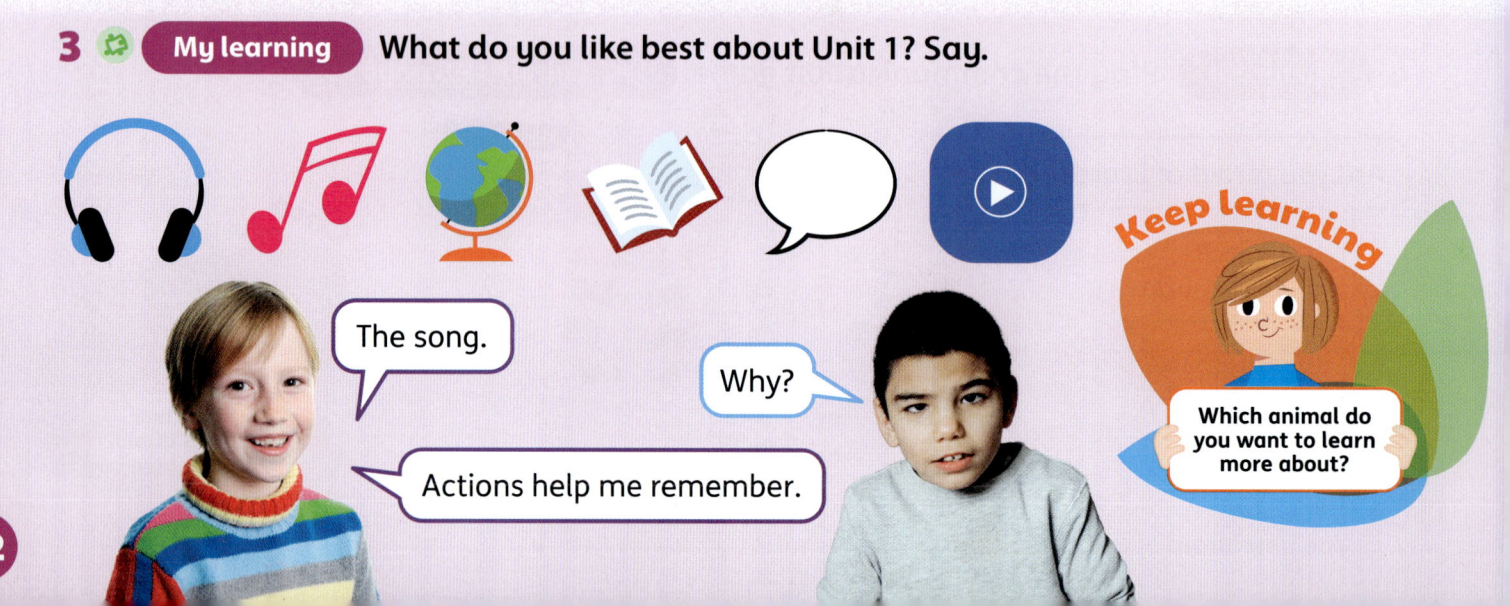

3. **My learning** What do you like best about Unit 1? Say.

- The song.
- Why?
- Actions help me remember.

Keep learning

Which animal do you want to learn more about?

12

Lesson 9 Project · Unit 1

The animal game

1 Work in groups of 3. Say.

What do we need?

Paper, pencils, colouring pens.

2 Read and do. Talk bank

1 Fold the paper into 3 parts.
Draw a head. Then fold and pass it on.

2 Draw a body and arms.
Then fold and pass it on.

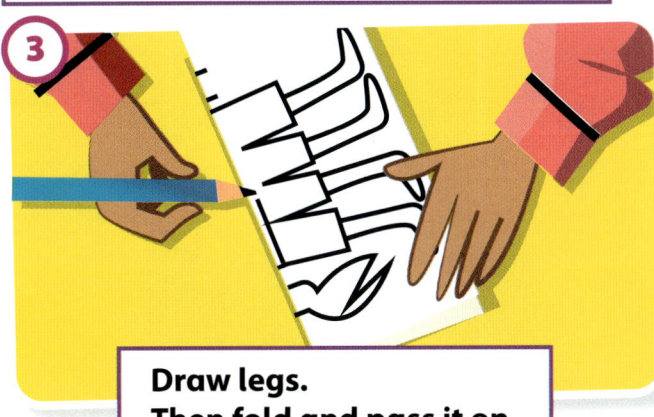

3 Draw legs.
Then fold and pass it on.

4 Open and colour the animal.

3 Mediation · Work in groups. Describe your animals.

It's funny. It's got a big head.

Is it friendly?

Video

13

Lesson 1 Vocabulary

2 Bedroom

Video 1 Remember the things in the bedroom.

2 🔊 031 Listen, point and repeat. Say the number and the word.

3 🔊 032 Listen for the sounds. Listen and chant.

Pronunciation clock /ɒ/ photos /əʊ/

1 a bed	5 photos
2 a rug	6 speaker
3 an alarm clock	7 cushions
4 a guitar	8 lights

4 🔊 033 What's in Mia's bedroom? Listen and say.

5 🔊 034 Listen and repeat. Ask and answer.

Have you got a rug in your bedroom?

Yes, I have.

Connect What's your favourite thing in your bedroom?

Review Have you got … ? Yes, I have. No, I haven't.

14

Lesson 2 Grammar **Unit 2**

Video

1 🔊 035 Listen and read. Act it out.

1. Come in. Look! This is my new speaker. — It's cool.
2. And these are our new cushions. Sit down. — This isn't a cushion. It's a cat! — Miaow!

2 🔊 036 Listen, read and follow. Listen and repeat.

This is	my	speaker.
		rug.
These are	our	cushions.
		lights.

3 🔊 037 Listen and chant.

Look!

This is my speaker.

These are our lights.

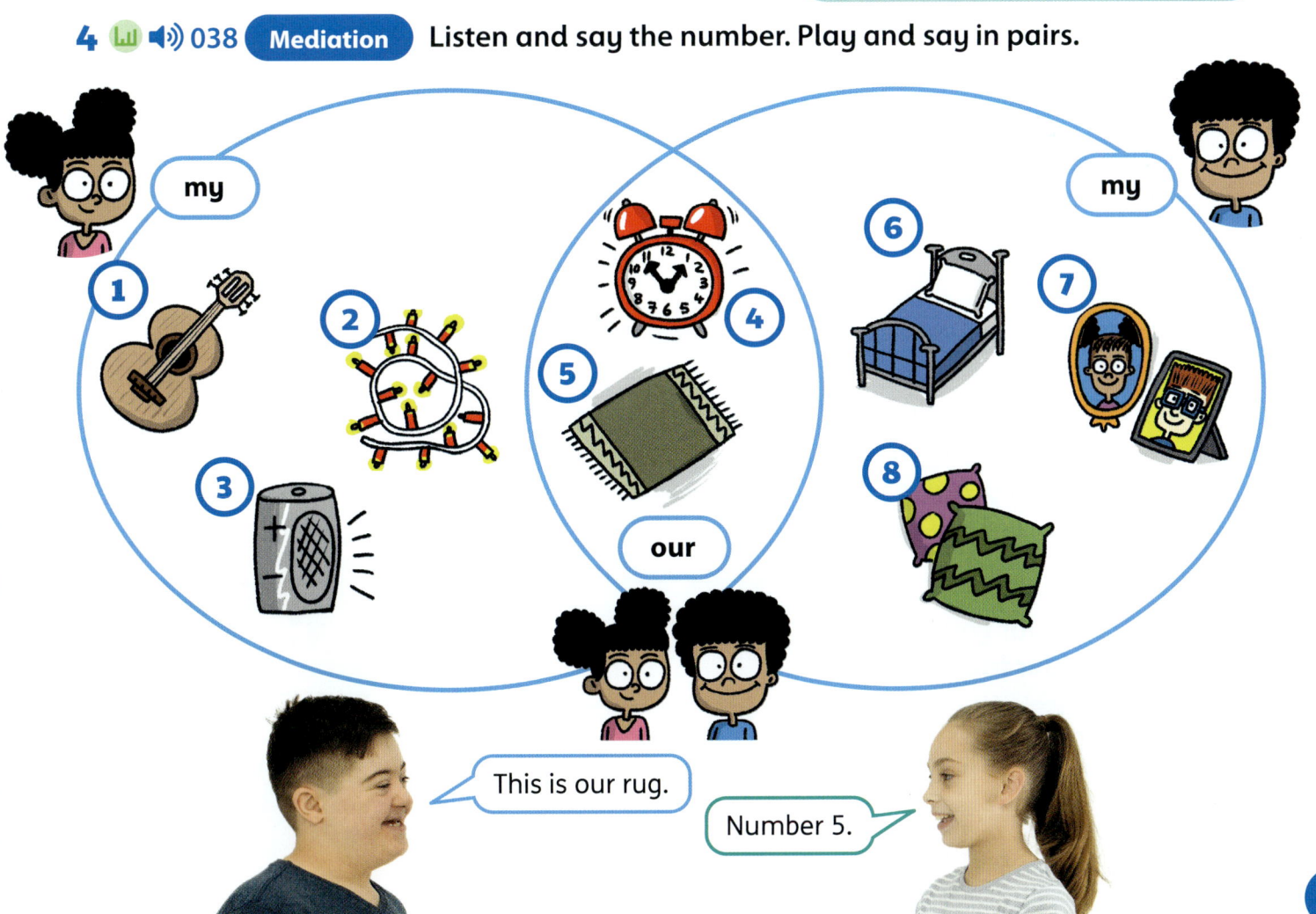

4 🔊 038 **Mediation** Listen and say the number. Play and say in pairs.

my

1. guitar
2. lights
3. speaker
4. clock
5. rug
6. bed
7. pictures
8. cushions

my

our

This is our rug.

Number 5.

15

Lesson 3 Song

▶ Video 1 🔊 040 Dance and move. Think about the song. Say.

I feel …   calm   happy   sad   sleepy

2 🔊 041 Listen, read and sing. Point and say the things *not* in the song.

Our room

*This is our room. This is our room.
The place we love, so come right in.*

And this is my cushion
and these are my photos.
This is my guitar,
I play when I feel sad.

*So this is our room. This is our room.
The place we love, so come right in.*

And these are our lights
I turn them on at night.
This is my bed,
where I read and sleep.

3 👥 Write new song lines. Change the words. ✏️

> And this is my …
> And these are my …
> This is my guitar,
> I play when I feel …

4 Create actions for your song. **Talk bank** ⬇
Perform for your friends.

I can mime *play the guitar*!   Well done!

Connect
Talk and listen.
Share your ideas.

16

Lesson 4 Culture | **Unit 2**

Where we sleep

Video **1** Where do children sleep in the video?

- on a futon
- in a hammock
- in a kitchen
- on a chair

2 Look and say what you see.

3 🔊 043 Listen and read. Point and say the **words**.

Hi, I'm Luc and this is my brother. We live in a flat in Paris, in France. We haven't got a garden but there's a **balcony**.

This is our bedroom. It's got a **rug** on the **floor**, a **desk** and a very colourful **chair**. We sleep in **bunk beds**. My bed is on **top**. There are five **lights** in our bedroom.

1 — top, bunk beds

2 — futons, floor

Our friends, Junko and Miki, are from Japan. They're sisters. They sleep on the floor, on **futons**. In the morning they put the futons in the cupboard. I like their bedroom. It's very calm.

4 Look and read again. Say *True* or *False*. Correct the false sentences.

1 There's a balcony at Luc's flat.
2 There are eight lights in Luc's bedroom.
3 Luc's desk is colourful.
4 Luc sleeps on a futon.
5 Luc likes Junko and Miki's bedroom.

5 🔊 044 Listen and repeat. Which is your favourite bedroom? Why?

My favourite room is room 1. I like the bunk beds!

17

An alien in my bedroom

1 🔊 046 Listen, point and repeat.

1 next to   2 in front of   3 between   4 behind   5 above

2 🔊 047 Listen and read. What does the alien think about Oscar's bedroom?

1
- Mum, what can I do?
- Play in your bedroom.
- My bedroom is boring.

2
- I can read my book …
- These cushions are nice.

3
- Hello!
- Hello!
- Is this a human bedroom? Wow!
- Yes, it is.

4
- Is there a bed in your bedroom?
- Yes, there is! It's here – in front of the window.

5
- What's this, above the rug?
- It's my hammock.
- I like it.

6
- Is there a hammock in your bedroom?
- No, there isn't. What's this?
- It's my alarm clock.

Lesson 5 Story & Vocabulary   Unit 2

7 And what's this, next to your alarm clock?
It's my speaker!

8 What's this between the cupboard and the door?
It's my guitar. You can play it.

9 Your bedroom is great!
Thank you. Smile …

10 Hi, Oscar. Careful! Your tablet is behind you.
Hi, Mum.
Thanks! I'm sorry. My bedroom isn't boring!

3 Read and match. Say the number and the letter.

1 It's in front of the window.
2 It's between the door and the cupboard.
3 It's above the rug.
4 It's next to the alarm clock.
5 It's on the cushions, behind Oscar.

4 Describe Oscar's bedroom. Share ideas and say.

It's colourful.   It's comfortable.   It isn't boring.
It's fun.   It's calm.

Take notice
What's good about your bedroom?

Review   bedroom   book   cupboard   door

19

Lesson 6 Story & Grammar

▶ Video **1** Story challenge Answer the questions.

2 🔊 048 Listen, look and answer. Say *A* or *B*.

A — Yes, there is.

B — No, there isn't.

3 🔊 049 Listen, read and follow. Listen and repeat.

?			+	−
Is there	a chair a rug an alarm clock an alien	in your bedroom?	Yes, there is.	No, there isn't.

Look!

an + a e i o u
an **a**larm clock

4 💬 Ask and answer about your bedroom.

5 🔊 050 Listen and say the number. Ask and answer.

Is there a rug in your bedroom?

No, there isn't.

1 2 3 4

20

Listen and speak

Lesson 7 Skills   Unit 2

1 Look and say what you see.

2 🔊 052 Listen and say the number. Where's the 🎸 and the 📻? Look and write. ✏️

3 🔊 053 Listen and read. Listen and repeat. Act out the dialogue.

- I'm sorry for breaking your guitar.
- Don't worry. Let's repair it.
- Good idea. Maybe my dad can help.

4 **Speak up!** Play the communication game. ✂ Cut-outs AB page 99

- I'm sorry for breaking your tablet.
- Don't worry!

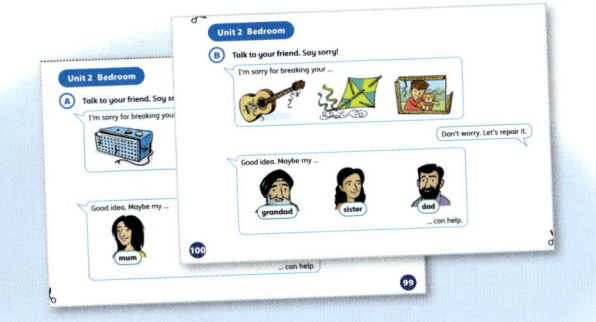

Care

Say sorry for breaking something.

I'm sorry for breaking …   Don't worry!

21

Lesson 8 Review

1 Play *Beat the clock* with your class.

Let's start. Number 1. Stand behind a friend.

OK. 1 point to you.

- 1 Stand behind a friend.
- 2 Make a true sentence. *This is my …*
- 3 Wave your hands in front of your head.
- 4 Ask and answer. *Is there a … in your bedroom?*
- 5 Stand between 2 friends.
- 6 Make a true sentence. *These are my …*
- 7 Put your bag under your chair.
- 8 Say 4 things in your bedroom.
- 9 Stand next to a friend.
- 10 Make a true sentence. *This is our …*
- 11 Wave your hands above your head.
- 12 Ask and answer. *Is there a … in your bedroom?*

2 Play the game with your friends. Which is your favourite challenge?

3 My learning What do you like best about Unit 2? Say.

Lesson 2 – grammar!

Why?

The video is funny and it helps me understand.

Keep learning

Can you describe another room in your house?

22

Lesson 9 Project | **Unit 2**

Design a bedroom

1 Work in groups. Say.

What do we need?

We need card, scissors, glue and coloured pens or pencils, material, magazines and pictures from the internet.

2 Read and do. **Talk bank**

1 What's in your bedroom? Share your ideas.

2 Look for pictures and cut them out. Draw pictures too.

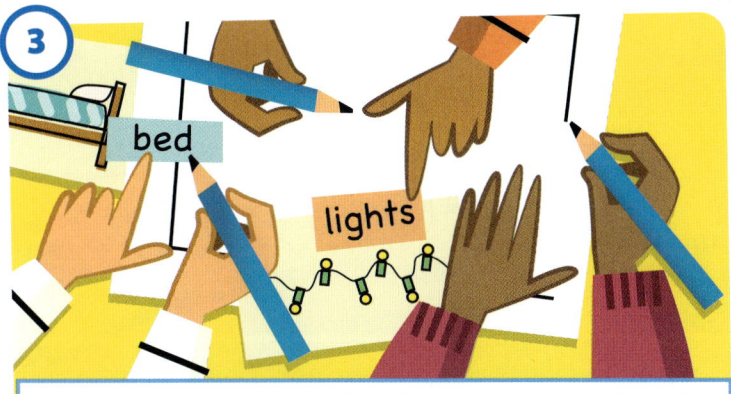

3 Draw a big room and write some word labels.

4 Create your bedroom. Stick the pictures and labels.

3 **Mediation** Work in groups. Describe your bedroom.

Our bedroom has got a hammock and cool cushions.

Is there a cupboard?

Yes, there is. It's next to the chair.

▶ Video

23

Channel challenge 1

Video 1 Look and say the words you know.

2 Write a list. Look, cover and say.

animals	bedroom	adjectives

3 054 Listen, find and answer.

4 Read, find and say. 055 Listen and check. Write.

This is my 🦂 .
It's ... the speaker.
It isn't friendly.
It's ... .

... are my 🦋 .
They're ... the cupboard.
They ... scary. They're ... .

scary   next to   scorpion

butterflies   aren't   These   above   colourful

24

Review Units 1–2
Learning situation

Hi! I'm Jack and this is my brother, Lee. This is our bedroom. We love animals.

5 Choose an animal. Describe and guess.

Talk bank

They're friendly. They aren't scary.

Are they green?

Yes, they are.

They're frogs.

6 Read and do.

Open Up **Learning situation**

What do we know about animals in danger? How can we help them? Create a class display.

Think — I know about …
I want to know about …

Research and prepare

How can you find out about animals in danger?

🖥 go online   📗 use a library   💬 ask a friend

Share your research and draw and write about animals in danger.

Present and share

Work together. Create your class display.

This is … 🦎 .
… on the … . It's friendly.
It … dangerous.

isn't   It's   our   rug   lizard

7 Read, think and say.

Keep learning

What's your best work in Units 1 and 2?

What can you improve in Units 3 and 4?

Learn from your mistakes.

Lesson 1 Vocabulary

3 Dressing up

Video 1 Remember the clothes.

2 🔊 057 Listen, point and repeat. Say the number and the word.

3 🔊 058 Listen for the sounds. Listen and chant.

Pronunciation hair /eə/ beard /ɪə/

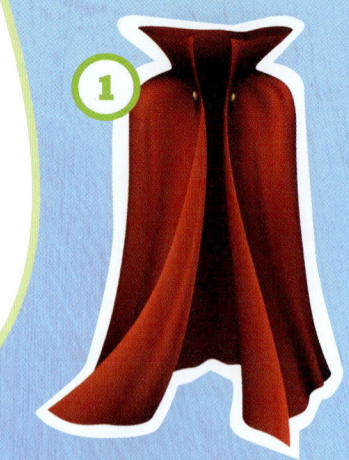

1 a cape	5 a wig
2 a necklace	6 sunglasses
3 a beard	7 boots
4 a belt	8 sandals

4 🔊 059 Listen and say the dressing up things.

5 🔊 060 Listen and repeat. Describe and guess.

They're red. They're funny.

They're sunglasses.

Connect

What are your favourite dressing up clothes?

Review It's … They're …

26

Lesson 2 Grammar   Unit 3

Video

1 🔊 061 Listen and read. Act it out.

1
- Can you see Alex, Grandma?
- No. What's he wearing? Sunglasses?
- No. He isn't wearing sunglasses.

2
- He's wearing a wig.
- That's Alex? Wow!

2 🔊 062 Listen, read and follow. Listen and repeat.   **3** 🔊 063 Listen and chant.

?	What's	she	wearing?
		he	
+	She's	wearing	a wig.
	He's		boots.
−	She	isn't wearing	boots.
	He		a wig.

Look!
What is = What's
He is = He's
She is = She's

4 🔊 064 **Mediation** Listen and say the number. Ask, answer and guess in pairs.

1   2   3   4   5   6

- It's a girl.
- She's wearing a black cape and sandals. She isn't wearing a wig.
- What's she wearing?
- Number 4.

27

Lesson 3 Song

Video 1 🔊 066 Dance and move. Think about the song. Say.

I feel …   excited   energetic   calm   shy

2 🔊 067 Listen, read and sing. Say what the children are wearing.

The dressing up song

What's he wearing?
What's she wearing?
Is it something cool?
Hey! What's he wearing?
Hey! What's she wearing?
They look so cool.

He's wearing sunglasses,
A beard and a wig.
She's wearing dancing boots
And a cape. It's big!
And they look so cool!

She isn't wearing sandals and
He isn't wearing boots. (x2)

Anya
Josh
Varun
Kelly

3 Write new song lines. Change the words.

He's wearing … ,   She isn't wearing … and
A … and a wig.   He isn't wearing …
She's wearing …
And a … . It's big!

4 Create actions for your song. Talk bank
  Perform for your friends.

Let's stamp our feet.   Yes, that's a great idea.

Care
Give kind feedback.

28

Lesson 4 Culture | **Unit 3**

Our dance clothes

Video 1 Which clothes can you remember from the video?

boots   skirt   trousers   sandals

Hi, I'm Dolkar and I'm from Ladakh in India. I'm learning about dance clothes.

2 Look and say what you see.

3 🎧 069 Listen and read. Match. Say the number and the letter.

a

b headdress

c

1 This is a special dance for Family Day in Bali in Indonesia. This is Wayan in the front. She isn't wearing a dress. She's wearing a long orange skirt and she's got a colourful **headdress**.

2 These children are in Ukraine. They're doing a dance to celebrate their city. The girl in the green dress is called Lena. She's wearing white socks and sandals. I think her dress is good for dancing.

This is a special dance to celebrate our city.

3 These are my friends in Ladakh. Can you see my brother, Dorje? He's wearing a necklace and black boots. He's got a red hat.

4 Look and read again. Say *True* or *False*. Correct the false sentences. 📝

1 Wayan is wearing a dress.
2 Dorje is wearing black boots.
3 Dorje isn't wearing a necklace.
4 Lena is wearing sandals.
5 Lena is wearing yellow socks.

5 👥 Which dance clothes do you like best? Why?

I like the headdress. It's colourful.   I like the boots.

29

Dressing up day

Video 1 🔊 071 Listen, point and repeat.

1 sparkly   2 stripy   3 spotty   4 flowery   5 beautiful   6 plain

2 🔊 072 Listen and read. What do Felipe and Maya make?

1
- Bye, Maya. Don't forget it's dressing up day tomorrow!
- Err … yes. Bye, Felipe!
- See you later! I can show you my costume! It's fantastic!

2 Later, at home.
- Look, I'm wearing a stripy T-shirt, a belt, a cape and boots.
- What colour is your costume, Maya?
- Err …

3
- Sonia's wearing a wig and she's got a brown beard.
- It's green. It's sparkly.
- What colour is her wig?

4
- Katya's wearing sunglasses, a red necklace and flowery trousers.
- What colour are her sunglasses?

5
- They're blue and yellow. They're spotty!
- Hey Maya. Are you OK? What's the matter?
- I haven't got a costume.

6
- You're wearing your butterfly T-shirt … I've got an idea!
- Perfect! I'm coming now …
- And plain black trousers.

30

Lesson 5 Story & Vocabulary   **Unit 3**

7 Come on. Let's make some sparkly wings.

OK. Pass me the pens, please!

8 The next day at school. It's dressing up day.

The winner is …

9 The butterfly! Maya's wings are beautiful! So sparkly and colourful.

10 Thank you, Felipe! You're a good friend.

You're welcome, Maya! You're a good friend, too!

3 Read and match. Say true sentences.

1 Katya's sunglasses …
2 Sonia's wig …
3 Maya's trousers …
4 Felipe's T-shirt …
5 Katya's trousers …

a
b
c 
d
e

is sparkly.
are flowery.
are plain.
is stripy.
are spotty.

4 How is Felipe a good friend to Maya? Share ideas and say.

He notices she is sad.   He listens to her.

He's kind.   He talks to her.   He helps her make wings.

Care

How can you be a good friend?

Review basket   lizard   trousers   wings

31

Lesson 6 Story & Grammar

▶ Video **1** Story challenge Answer the questions.

2 🔊 073 Listen, look and answer. 🔊 074 Listen and check.

Felipe · Sonia · Katya · Maya

What colour is … ?

What colour are … ?

3 🔊 075 Listen, read and follow. Listen and repeat. Ask and answer about Maya.

What colour	is	Felipe's / his	T-shirt? / belt?
	are	Katya's / her	sunglasses? / trousers?

Look!
Felipe's bag = his bag
Katya's bag = her bag

4 🗣 Ask and answer about your friends.

5 🔊 076 Listen and say the name. Describe and guess.

1. Kai
2. Ahmed
3. Misa
4. Lee
5. Erin
6. Taylor

His sunglasses are stripy.

What colour are his sandals?

They're brown. They're plain.

It's Kai.

32

Listen and speak

Lesson 7 Skills | **Unit 3**

1 Look and say what you see.

2 🔊 **078** Listen and say the number. Write a list of the clothes. ✏️

3 🔊 **079** Listen and read. Listen and repeat. Act out the dialogue.

- I've got a new bag.
- Oh, what's it like?
- It's green and black. It's got a picture of a frog.
- That sounds nice!

4 👥 **Speak up!** Play the communication game. ✂️ **Cut-outs AB page 101**

- I've got a new T-shirt.
- What's it like?
- It's stripy.
- That sounds nice!

I've got a … What's it like?

Care
Can you say something nice to your friend?

33

Lesson 8 Review

Video

1 Play *Three in a row* with your class.

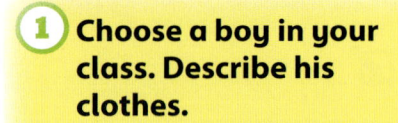

1. Choose a boy in your class. Describe his clothes.
   - He's wearing ...

2. Say 4 clothes for dressing up.

3. Describe this T-shirt.

4. Ask and answer about this boy.
   - What colour is his ... ? 
   - What colour are his ... ?

5. Answer the secret question.

6. Ask and answer about this girl. 
   - What colour is her ... ?
   - What colour are her ... ?

7. Describe these socks.

8. Say 4 things you wear to school.

9. Choose a girl in your class. Describe her clothes.
   - She's wearing ...

2 Make up your secret question. Play the game with your friends.

3 **My learning** What do you like best about Unit 3? Say.

- The guessing game.
- Why?
- Games are fun.

Keep learning

Can you learn more clothes words?

34

Lesson 9 Project | **Unit 3**

Our dressing up design

1 Work in groups of 3. Say.

— What do we need?

— We need paper, scissors, glue, old plastic bags, wrapping paper, card …

2 💡 Read and do. **Talk bank** ⬇

1 Share your dressing up design ideas!

2 Use the template. ⬇ Cut out, draw and colour your costume …

3 Or make the costume from different materials.

4 Stick and label your dressing up costume.

3 **Mediation** Work in groups. Ask and answer about your design.

— This is our dressing up design. What's she wearing?

— She's wearing a wig, a cape and …

— What colour is her T-shirt?

— It's orange, yellow and red. It's stripy.

▶ Video

35

4 Fun

Lesson 1 Vocabulary

Video 1 Remember the activities.

2 🔊 080 Listen, point and repeat. Say the number and the word.

3 🔊 081 Listen for the sounds. Listen and chant.

Pronunciation play /eɪ/   chat /æ/

1. play tennis
2. go swimming
3. do karate
4. play games
5. listen to music
6. make models
7. chat to friends
8. visit my grandparents

4 🔊 082 Listen and say the number.

5 🔊 083 Listen and repeat. Play a memory game.

I play tennis on Monday …

I play tennis on Monday and I do karate on Tuesday …

Take notice
What do you do to feel happy?

Review Days of the week

36

Lesson 2 Grammar · **Unit 4**

Video · 1 🔊 084 Listen and read. Act it out.

1 — What do you do at the weekend, Teo?
— I go swimming on Saturday – with Grandad.

2 — What do you do on Sunday?
— I don't go swimming. I visit Grandad – and I do karate!

2 🔊 085 Listen, read and follow. Listen and repeat.   **3** 🔊 086 Listen and chant.

?	+	-
What do you do …	I play games.	I don't play games.
… at the weekend?	I make models.	I don't make models.
… on Monday?	I go to school.	

Look! don't = do not

4 🔊 087 **Mediation** Listen and say the name. Ask, answer and guess in pairs.

	Sam	Leah	Lucas	Marta
Saturday				
Sunday				

— What do you do at the weekend?
— I do karate on Saturday. I listen to music on Sunday. I don't do karate on Sunday.
— You're Lucas.

37

Lesson 3 Song

Video

1 🔊 089 Dance and move. Think about the song. Say.

I feel …   calm   happy   upset   excited

2 🔊 090 Listen, read and sing. Which activities in the song do *you* do at the weekend?

My weekend

What do you do at the weekend?
What do you do all day?
What do you do at the weekend?
On Saturday and Sunday?

I play football. I make models
And I do karate.
I chat to my friends
And maybe go to a party,

But I don't visit Grandma
And I don't visit Grandad
Because they live far away …

3 Write new song lines. Change the words.

> I play …, I …
> And I do karate.
> I …
> And maybe go to a party,

4 Create actions for your song. **Talk bank**
Perform for your friends.

Let's kick our legs!   Good idea!

Take part

Listen and join in.

38

Lesson 4 Culture **Unit 4**

Martial arts

▶ **Video** **1** Which activities are in the video?

taekwondo swimming karate football

Hi. I'm Sung-ho and I'm from South Korea. I love martial arts. Taekwondo is from Korea!

2 🟢 Look and say what you see.

3 🔊 092 Listen and read. Match. Say the number and the letter.

a

1 Lots of children learn martial arts. This is Do-yun. He's learning taekwondo. He's a beginner. He's got a white belt. His teacher is helping him. His teacher is very good at taekwondo. He's got a black belt.

b

2 I do taekwondo at the weekend. Liam and Katy do taekwondo at the weekend, too. They've got red belts now. Look, Katy is doing a high kick. She's shouting, too.

c kick

still

3 Martial arts are very energetic and they can make you feel strong and brave. They can help you feel calm, too. These girls are very quiet and still.

4 Read, choose A or B and say true sentences. 📝 Then write.

1 Do-yun has got a	A white belt.	B black belt.
2 His teacher has got a	A red belt.	B black belt.
3 Taekwondo comes from	A Japan.	B Korea.
4 Liam and Katy do taekwondo	A on Monday.	B at the weekend.
5 Martial arts can help you feel	A calm.	B shy.

5 👥 What do you like about martial arts? Think of more ideas and say.

They're energetic.   You can kick and shout.

39

Eva's busy day

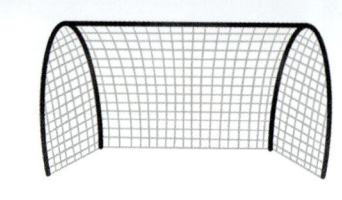

Video

1 🔊 095 Listen, point and repeat.

1 before school   2 after school   3 at break   4 at lunchtime
5 in the morning   6 in the afternoon

2 🔊 096 Listen and read. What is Eva's new favourite activity?

1 Great. It's Monday. I do ALL my favourite activities.
Yes! It's the big football match after school today.

2 I do karate before school. Let's go.
Do you do karate before school, Frank?
No, I don't.

3 Great, it's break! I play tennis at break. See you later.
Oh!

4 It's lunchtime. I'm hungry.
I do music club at lunchtime. My lunch is in my bag.

5 Later, at model club in the afternoon.
Do you play football after school, Eva?
Yes, I do. Oh, the football match!

6 OK, Eva. You can go in goal.
Sorry I'm late, Mr Chen.

40

Lesson 5 Story & Vocabulary **Unit 4**

7 "Oh, no Eva! Wake up!"
"He's coming now! He's got the ball!"

8 "NO!"
"Noooo!"
"I'm sorry everyone!"

9 After the game.
"You do too many things! You're tired."
"You're our friend, but we don't see you."

10 Next Monday in the morning.
"Hi Eva. Do you do karate before school?"
"No, I don't, Mum! I've got a new favourite activity ... chatting to my friends!"

3 Make true sentences for Eva. Match and say. ♻ Make true sentences for you.

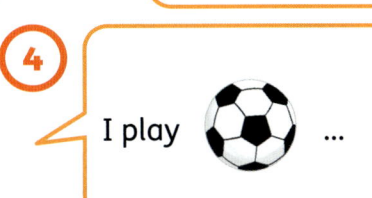

1. I do ♪ club ...
2. I play 🎾 ...
3. I do 🥋 ...
4. I play ⚽ ...

a after school.
b at break.
c before school.
d at lunchtime.

4 How do Eva and her friends feel? Share ideas and say.

upset   happy   excited
tired   worried   energetic

Care
Make time for your friends.

Review bag   cushions   play football   speaker

41

Lesson 6 Story & Grammar

▶ Video **1** Story challenge Answer the questions.

2 🔊 097 Listen and answer for Eva.

My day by Eva

| in the morning | in the afternoon |

Yes, I do.

No, I don't.

3 🔊 098 Listen, read and follow. Listen and repeat. **4** Ask and answer with your friend.

?		+	-
Do you	play tennis do karate make models play football	at the weekend?	Yes, I do.	No, I don't.

Look!
in the …
morning
afternoon

at the weekend
on Monday

5 🔊 099 Listen, look and say the name. Ask, answer and guess.

Frank's weekend   Eva's weekend   Mr Chen's weekend

Do you read a book at the weekend?

Yes, I do.

Do you listen to music?

No, I don't.

Are you Mr Chen?

Yes, I am.

42

Listen and speak

Lesson 7 Skills | **Unit 4**

1 Look and say what you see. Do you do the activities?

2 🔊 101 Listen and say the number. When does Amina play her guitar? Write. ✏️

3 🔊 102 Listen and read. Listen and repeat. Act out the dialogue.

— What do you like doing in your free time?

— I like playing football. What about you? Do you like playing football?

— Yes, I do. I like playing tennis, too.

4 ♻️ **Speak up!** Play the communication game. ✂️ **Cut-outs AB page 101**

— What do you like doing in your free time?

— I like reading.

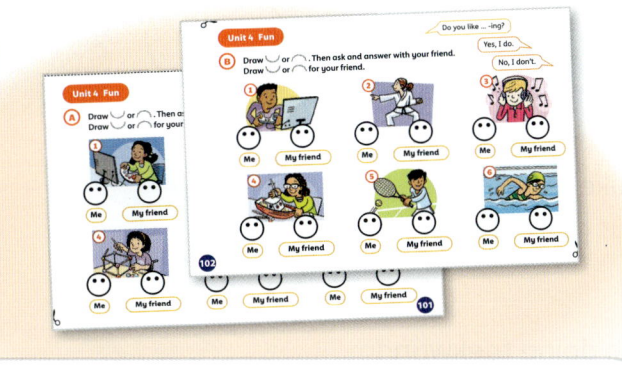

Take part

What do you like doing?

What do you like doing in your free time?   I like … ing.   What about you?

43

Lesson 8 Review

Video   **1** Play *Beat the clock* with your class.

Let's start. Number 1. Say 3 activities.

read a book, play football, play games

Wheel:
1. Say the activities.
2. Ask. … you … making models … weekend?
3. What do you do at the weekend? Say 5 things.
4. Say. I … on Monday.
5. Say the days of the week.
6. Ask. … read a book … break?
7. What do you do after school? Say 3 things.
8. Say. I don't … at the weekend.
9. Say 2 martial arts.
10. Ask. … you play games … lunchtime?
11. What do you like doing? Say 5 things.
12. Say. I … in the morning.

2 Play the game with your friends. Which is your favourite challenge?

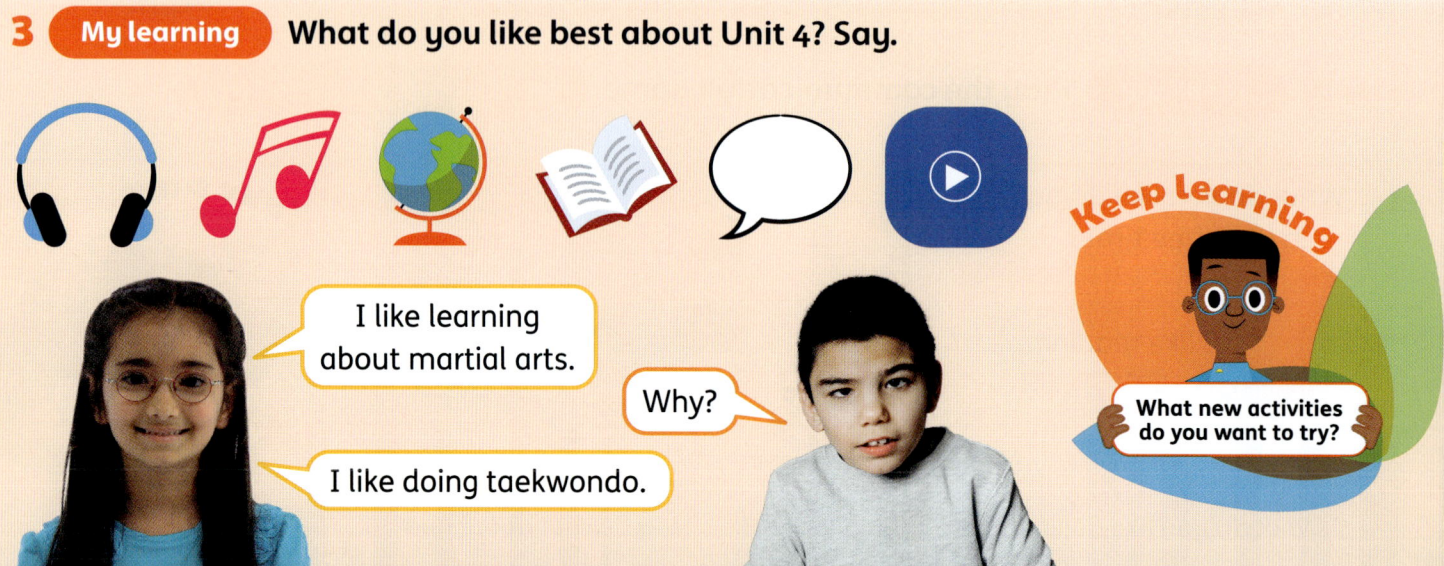

3 **My learning** What do you like best about Unit 4? Say.

I like learning about martial arts.

Why?

I like doing taekwondo.

Keep learning

What new activities do you want to try?

44

Lesson 9 Project | **Unit 4**

The fun game

1 Work in groups of 4. Say.

— What do we need?
— We need scissors, a ruler, glue, coloured pens or pencils, counters ...

2 Read and do. **Talk bank**

1 Think of activities you do for fun.

2 Draw or stick pictures of three activities on the template.

3 Write times for the activities on the template.

4 Stick your squares together on card to make a game board. Write start and finish.

3 **Mediation** Work in groups. Play the game.

— Do you play tennis on Monday?
— No, I don't.
— Yes, I do. OK, your turn.

= 1 move   = 2 moves

▶ Video

45

Channel challenge 2

▶ Video **1** Look and say the words you know.

2 Write a list. Look, cover and say.

animals	bedroom	clothes	activities

3 Ask and answer about Stan and Sara's clothes.

What's he wearing?

What's she wearing?

What colour are her sandals?

Super Stan

Super Sara

4 Read, look and say. 🔊 103 Listen and check. Write.

Super Stan's wearing … , a … and a … .
He isn't wearing a … . His trousers are … .

wig   cape   boots   belt   plain

Super Sara isn't wearing a … or … .
She's wearing … trousers and green … . Her cape is … .

stripy   spotty   sunglasses
belt   sandals

46

Review Units 3–4
Learning situation

Interview

What do you do on Friday, Stan?
I …
What do you do at the weekend?
On Saturday I …
Do you … on Sunday?
No, I don't. I …

5 Read the interview. Say the missing words. Plan and act out an interview with Sara.

Talk bank

What do you do on Tuesday, Super Sara?

I go to school.

	Super Stan	Super Sara
Monday Tuesday Wednesday Thursday Friday		
Saturday		
Sunday		

6 Read and do.

Open Up — Learning situation

Who are your heroes? Create a poster.

Think
I know about …
I want to know about …

Research and prepare
How can you find out about heroes?
 go online   use a library   ask a friend
Share your research and make your poster.

Present and share
Work together. Present your poster to the class.

7 Read, think and say.

What's your best work in Units 3 and 4?
What can you improve in Units 5 and 6?

Keep learning
Keep trying and do your best.

47

Lesson 1 Vocabulary

5 Food

▶ **Video** 1 Remember the food.

2 🔊 105 Listen, point and repeat. Say the number and the word.

3 🔊 106 Listen for the sounds. Listen and chant.

| Pronunciation | grapes /s/ | sandwiches /iz/ | peppers /z/ |

1 crisps
2 yoghurt
3 sandwiches
4 lemons
5 biscuits
6 grapes
7 apples
8 peppers

4 🔊 107 Listen, point and do 👍 or 👎.

5 🔊 108 Listen and repeat. Ask and answer.

Do you like yoghurt?
Yes, I do.

Do you like crisps?
No, I don't.

Take notice
We say *Thank you* for our food.

Review Do you like … ? Yes, I do. No, I don't.

48

Lesson 2 Grammar | Unit 5

Video

1 🔊 109 Listen and read. Act it out.

1. Does he like apples? — No, he doesn't.
2. Does she like grapes? — No, she doesn't.
3. Does he like grapes? — Yes, he does. And she likes apples. Phew!

2 🔊 110 Listen, read and follow. Listen and repeat.   **3** 🔊 111 Listen and chant.

?			+	−
Does	she	like peppers? biscuits?	Yes, she does.	No, she doesn't.
	he	like sandwiches? lemons?	Yes, he does.	No, he doesn't.

Look!

doesn't = does not

4 🔊 112 **Mediation** Listen and say the number. Ask and answer in pairs.

Does he like sandwiches?
Yes, he does.
Number 4.

49

Lesson 3 Song

Video 1 🔊 114 Dance and move. Think about the song. Say.

I feel …   hungry   thirsty   excited   worried

2 🔊 115 Listen, read and sing. Describe the lunches. Who likes their lunch?

Lunchtime

What's she got for lunch? Let me see!
What's she got for lunch? I'm hungry!

A big, cheese sandwich,
Crisps and yoghurt.
Does she like yoghurt?
Yes, she does!

What's he got for lunch? Let me see!
What's he got for lunch? I'm hungry!

A pizza with peppers,
Biscuits and grapes.
Does he like grapes?
No, he doesn't!

Elena   Ken   Luis

3 👥 Write new song lines. Change the words. ✎

> A pizza with … ,
> … and …
> Does he like … ?
> …

4 Create actions for your song. **Talk bank** Perform for your friends.

Let's clap our hands!
And stamp our feet!
Great idea!

50

Lesson 4 Culture   **Unit 5**

A cherry festival

Video **1** What food can you see in the video?

apples   sandwiches   cake   ice cream

Hello. My name's Rada and I'm from Bulgaria. There's a cherry festival in my town in summer.

2 Look and say what you see.

3 🔊 117 Listen and read. Match. Say the number and the letter.

a cherries

1 This is me and my sister Sofia. We've got a basket of cherries and we've got cherries on our ears. We like cherries! Do you like cherries? They're sweet and sour!

b

2 There are lots of cherries at the festival. Look! They're different colours. They're red, yellow and orange. People make beautiful pictures with the cherries. Look at this flower.

c basket

3 There's a holiday for the festival and we don't go to school. These women are wearing special clothes. We all eat lots of cherries!

4 Look and read again. Say *True* or *False*. Correct the false sentences.

1 The cherry festival is in winter.
2 You can make pictures with cherries.
3 Rada and Sofia have got cherries on their eyes.
4 You can see yellow cherries at the festival.
5 Rada and Sofia go to school on the festival day.
6 Rada doesn't like cherries.

5 🟢 👥 What food do you celebrate with? Make a picture list.

cake – on my birthday

Connect
What other food festivals do you know?

51

The rude queen

Prince Antony

Queen Antya

Video

1 🔊 119 Listen, point and repeat.

| 1 sweet | 2 salty | 3 sour | 4 spicy | 5 hard | 6 soft |

2 🔊 120 Listen and read. Does Queen Antya change in the story?

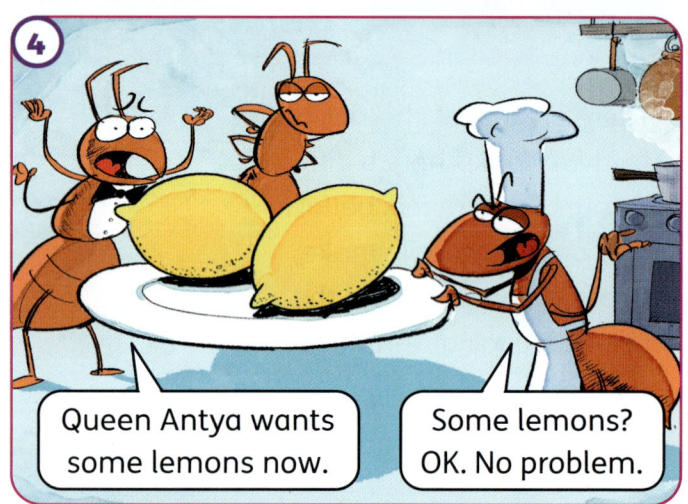

1 At the ant palace …
I'm hungry! I want some food. Where's our lunch?

2 Does he like peppers?
Yes, he does.
Does she like peppers?

3 No, she doesn't.
Agh! These peppers are very spicy. I want some lemons.

4 Queen Antya wants some lemons now.
Some lemons? OK. No problem.

5 Great. Thank you.
Yuk! These lemons are very sour. I don't want any lemons.
She doesn't want any lemons.

6 She doesn't want any biscuits … or any apples … or any bread.
Yuk! Too sweet!
Too hard!
This bread is very soft.

52

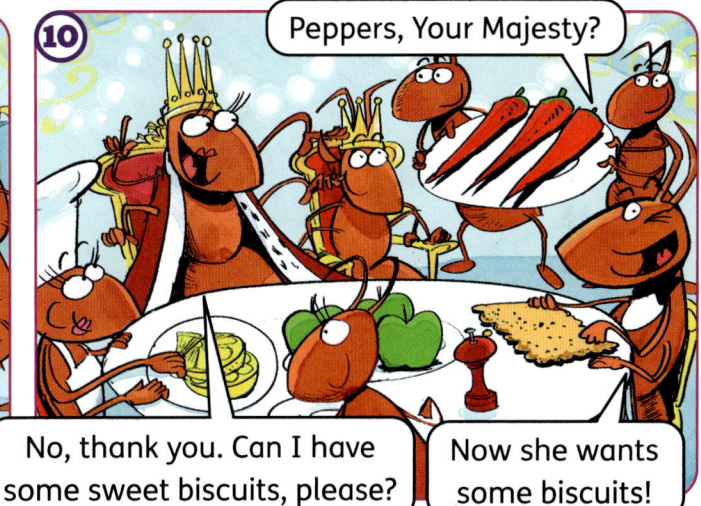

Lesson 5 Story & Vocabulary **Unit 5**

7
- Some crisps, Your Majesty?
- Yuk! No! They're too salty.
- That's it! You're rude. Goodbye!

8
- It's true. You ARE rude. You don't say *Please* or *Thank you*.
- Wait … please!

9
- My dear Ants. I'm sorry!
- Let's ALL have lunch together, please?

10
- Peppers, Your Majesty?
- No, thank you. Can I have some sweet biscuits, please?
- Now she wants some biscuits!

3 Read and say true sentences about the story. Then write.

1 The peppers  are spicy salty .

2 The apples  are soft hard .

3 The bread 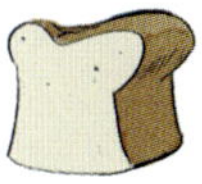 is soft spicy .

4 The lemons  are sweet sour .

5 The biscuits  are sweet spicy .

6 The crisps  are salty sour .

4 Describe the ants! Share ideas and say.

He's …
She's …

friendly   calm   rude

funny   kind   angry

Take notice

How do you feel when someone is rude? How do you feel when someone is kind?

Review bread   cape   dining room   lights

53

Lesson 6 Story & Grammar

▶ Video 1 **Story challenge** Answer the questions.

2 🔊 121 Listen and say A, B, C or D. Say the missing food.

A She wants some …
B She doesn't want any …
C He wants some …
D He doesn't want any …

3 🔊 122 Listen, read and follow. Listen and repeat.

+	He / She	wants	some	crisps. apples.
−	He / She	doesn't want	any	lemons. peppers.

Look!
Ask politely!
Can I have some … , please?

4 Make true sentences about Queen Antya and Prince Antony.

5 🔊 123 Listen and say the number. Describe and guess.

She doesn't want any soft grapes.

Number 3.

54

Listen and speak

Lesson 7 Skills **Unit 5**

1 Look and say what you see. Which food do you like?

2 🔊 125 Listen and say the number.

① ②  ③  ④

3 🔊 126 Listen and read. Listen and repeat. Act out the dialogue.

- What time is it?
- It's one o'clock. It's lunchtime.
- What have you got for lunch?
- I've got cheese and pepper sandwiches. I love spicy peppers. What about you?

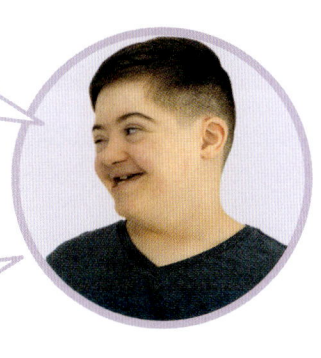

4 **Speak up!** Play the communication game. ✂ **Cut-outs AB page 103**

- What time is it?
- It's two o'clock. It's lunchtime.
- What have you got for lunch?
- I've got ...

Connect

What do you like about meal times?

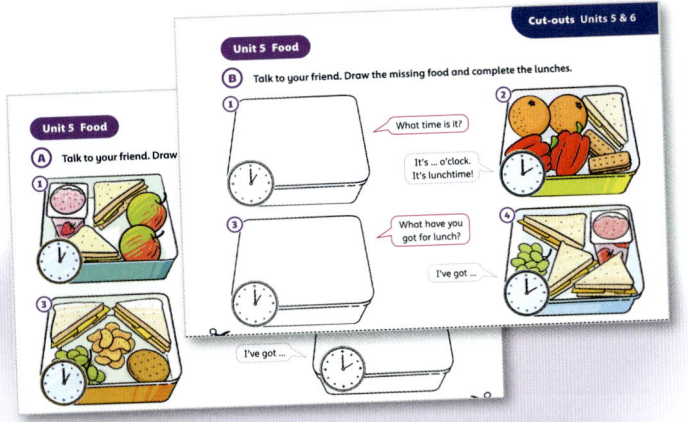

What time is it? It's lunchtime. What have you got for lunch?

55

Lesson 8 Review

Video 1 Play *Three in a row* with your class.

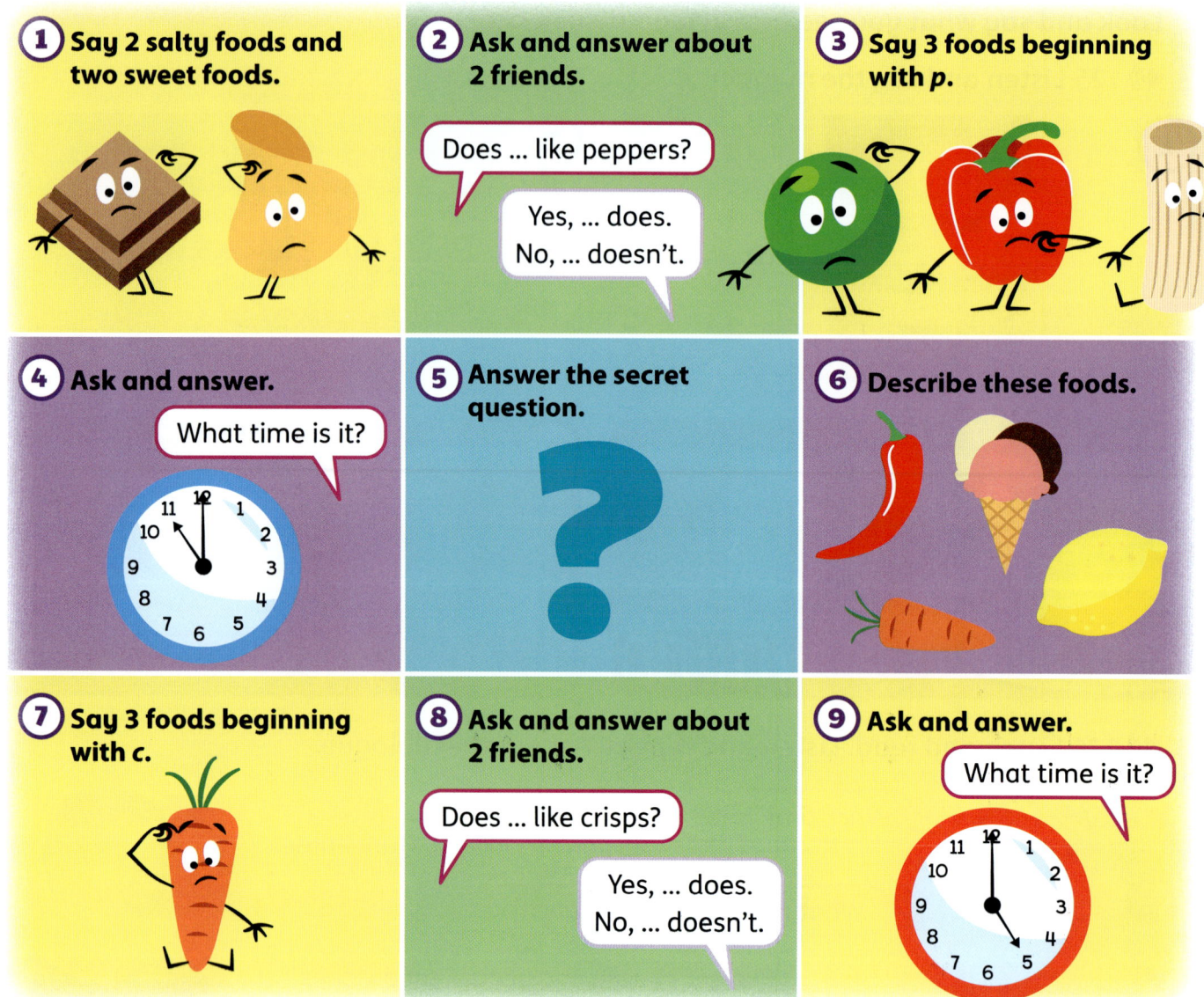

1. Say 2 salty foods and two sweet foods.

2. Ask and answer about 2 friends.
   Does ... like peppers?
   Yes, ... does.
   No, ... doesn't.

3. Say 3 foods beginning with *p*.

4. Ask and answer.
   What time is it?

5. Answer the secret question.

6. Describe these foods.

7. Say 3 foods beginning with *c*.

8. Ask and answer about 2 friends.
   Does ... like crisps?
   Yes, ... does.
   No, ... doesn't.

9. Ask and answer.
   What time is it?

2 Make up your secret question. Play the game with your friends.

3 **My learning** What do you like best about Unit 5? Say.

The story.
Why?
I like reading stories.

Keep learning
Don't worry about making mistakes.

56

Perform a play

Lesson 9 Project — **Unit 5**

1 Work in groups of 4. Say.

"What do we need?"

"We need the play script, pens, scissors, masks, a crown and ideas!"

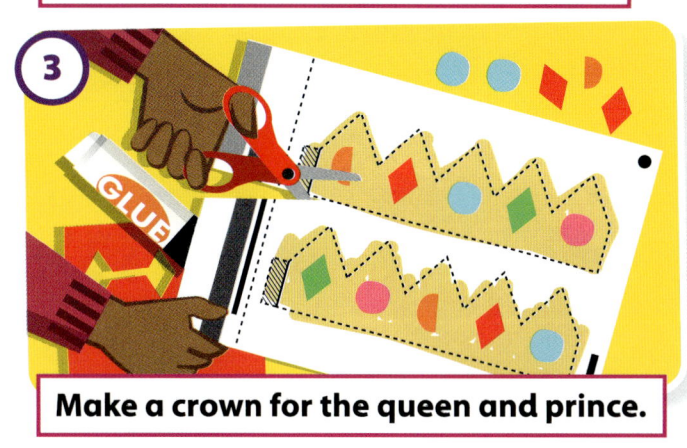

2 Read and do. **Talk bank**

1 "She wants some ice cream!" "I want to be the queen!"

Discuss ideas. Write your play on the template. Choose a character.

2 **Make masks for the ants.**

3 **Make a crown for the queen and prince.**

4 **Practise the play.**

3 **Mediation** Work in groups. Act out your play for your class.

"Bring me some ice cream. Yuk! It's very soft!"

"She doesn't want any ice cream! Does she like grapes?"

▶ Video

57

6 Entertainers

Lesson 1 Vocabulary

▶ **Video** 1 Remember the skills.

2 🔊 127 Listen, point and repeat. Say the number and the word.

3 🔊 128 Listen for the sounds. Listen and chant.

| Pronunciation | yellow /y/ | jump /dʒ/ |

1 do a handstand
2 juggle
3 do a somersault
4 do a cartwheel
5 balance
6 play the trumpet
7 stand still
8 walk a tightrope

4 🔊 129 Listen and mime.

5 🔊 130 Listen and repeat. Ask and answer.

Can you juggle?

Yes, I can.

Take part

What can you do to be active?

Review Can you … ? Yes, I can. No, I can't.

58

Lesson 2 Grammar | **Unit 6**

1 🔊 131 Listen and read. Act it out.

1
Can she walk a tightrope?
Yes, she can.

2
I'm fine. Don't worry.
Can he walk a tightrope?
Oops. No, he can't.

2 🔊 132 Listen, read and follow. Listen and repeat.   **3** 🔊 133 Listen and chant.

		?	+	-
Can	she	do a somersault? do a handstand?	Yes, she can.	No, she can't.
	he	stand still? walk a tightrope?	Yes, he can.	No, he can't.

Look!
can't = can not

4 🔊 134 **Mediation** Listen, find and answer. Ask and answer in pairs.

Number 8. Can he do a cartwheel?

Yes, he can.

59

Lesson 3 Song

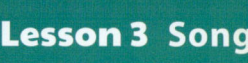

Video 1 🔊 136 Dance and move. Think about the song. Say.

I feel … | energetic | excited | scared | tired | strong

2 🔊 137 Listen, read and sing. What can you do?

Different things

Can she balance? No, she can't.
Can she walk a tightrope? No, she can't.
Can she do a somersault? No, she can't.
Can she play the trumpet? Yes, she can!

*We can all do different things.
What can you do?
We can all do different things.
So can you!*

Can he juggle? No, he can't.
Can he do a cartwheel? No, he can't.
Can he do a somersault? No, he can't.
Can he play the guitar? Yes, he can!

3 👥 Write new song lines. Change the words. ✏️

> Can he … ? No, he can't.
> Can he … ? No, he can't.
> Can he … ? No, he can't.
> Can he … ?
> YES, HE CAN!

4 💡 Create actions for your song.

Talk bank ⬇ Perform for your friends.

- I can mime *play the guitar*!
- Good idea!
- That's really good!

Keep learning

Encourage your friends and keep practising!

60

Lesson 4 Culture | **Unit 6**

The Edinburgh Festival

▶ **Video**   **1** What do the entertainers do in the video?

- juggle
- play music
- dance
- walk a tightrope

Hi. I'm Ravi and I'm from Edinburgh in Scotland. There's a big festival in Edinburgh in the summer.

2 🌐 Look and say what you see.

3 🔊 139 Listen and read. Match. Say the number and the letter.

a unicycle / wheel

1 There's lots to see at the Edinburgh Festival. Outdoor entertainers do lots of amazing things. Look at Kirsty. She can balance on one wheel. Her bike is called a unicycle.

b gold

2 Can you see Robbie? He's wearing a gold hat, a gold jacket, gold trousers and gold shoes. He can balance and stand very still. My friend Lucy is standing in front of Robbie. Lucy is trying to stand still, but it's difficult!

c

3 Here are some fantastic jugglers, Clare and Emma. They're in a park in Edinburgh. Clare is on top. She can balance and juggle. I can't juggle. Can you juggle?

4 Read, choose A or B and say true sentences. Then write. 📝

		A	B
1	The Edinburgh Festival is …	in winter.	in summer.
2	Robbie can …	stand still.	do a handstand.
3	Kirsty can balance on a …	unicycle	scooter.
4	Clare is in a park. She can …	juggle.	do a cartwheel.
5	Can Ravi juggle?	Yes, he can.	No, he can't.

5 👥 Who is your favourite entertainer? Why?

- I like Kirsty. She's …
- I like Robbie. I like his …

61

Where are the apples?

1 🔊 141 **Listen, point and repeat.**

1 dancer   2 juggler   3 musician   4 clown   5 acrobat   6 statue

2 🔊 142 **Listen and read. Which is your favourite entertainer?**

1
At the festival.
Look at the dancers. And the musician!
I'm hungry. Can I have an apple please, Leila?

2
Where are the apples?
There's an acrobat. He can do a somersault.

3
Amazing! He can do a cartwheel very well – with one hand!
Hmm! Apples!
I can do a cartwheel quite well.

4
He can't play the trumpet very well.
There's a clown! He's got the apples in his trumpet.

5
The clown is throwing the apples to the juggler.

6
Wow. She can juggle very well.
I can't juggle.

62

Lesson 5 Story & Vocabulary | Unit 6

7 Look at the statue. She can stand very still!

8 Look, Leila! She's moving! She's got the apples! She's eating one!

9 But Ali! She's a statue. She can't move. She can't eat.

Thank you. What a delicious apple!

No problem.

10 I'm a living statue. These are my friends. Have an apple.

Wow! Thanks!

You're welcome.

3 Read, match and say. Then write.

1 Who can do a somersault?
2 Who can stand still?
3 Who can dance?
4 Who can juggle?
5 Who can't play the trumpet?

4 Talk about the entertainers. Which one do you like best? Share ideas and say.

I like the clown because he's …

funny   strong   brave

kind   energetic   still

Keep learning

What skill would you like to try?

Review apples bananas hand water bottle

63

Lesson 6 Story & Grammar

Video 1 **Story challenge** Answer the questions.

2 Read, look and say the name. 🔊 143 Listen and check.

Ryan   Ezra   Harlie

Aisha   Layla   Finn

1 He can do a handstand very well.
2 He can do a cartwheel quite well.
3 She can't do a handstand.
4 He can juggle very well.
5 She can't walk a tightrope very well.
6 She can't balance very well.

3 🔊 144 Listen, read and follow. Listen and repeat.   4 Tell your friend about your skills.

+	I / You / He	can	balance / juggle / stand still	very well. / quite well.
−	She / We / They	can't	do a handstand / walk a tightrope / play the trumpet	very well.

Look!
I can't juggle very well.

5 🔊 145 Listen and say the number. Describe and guess.

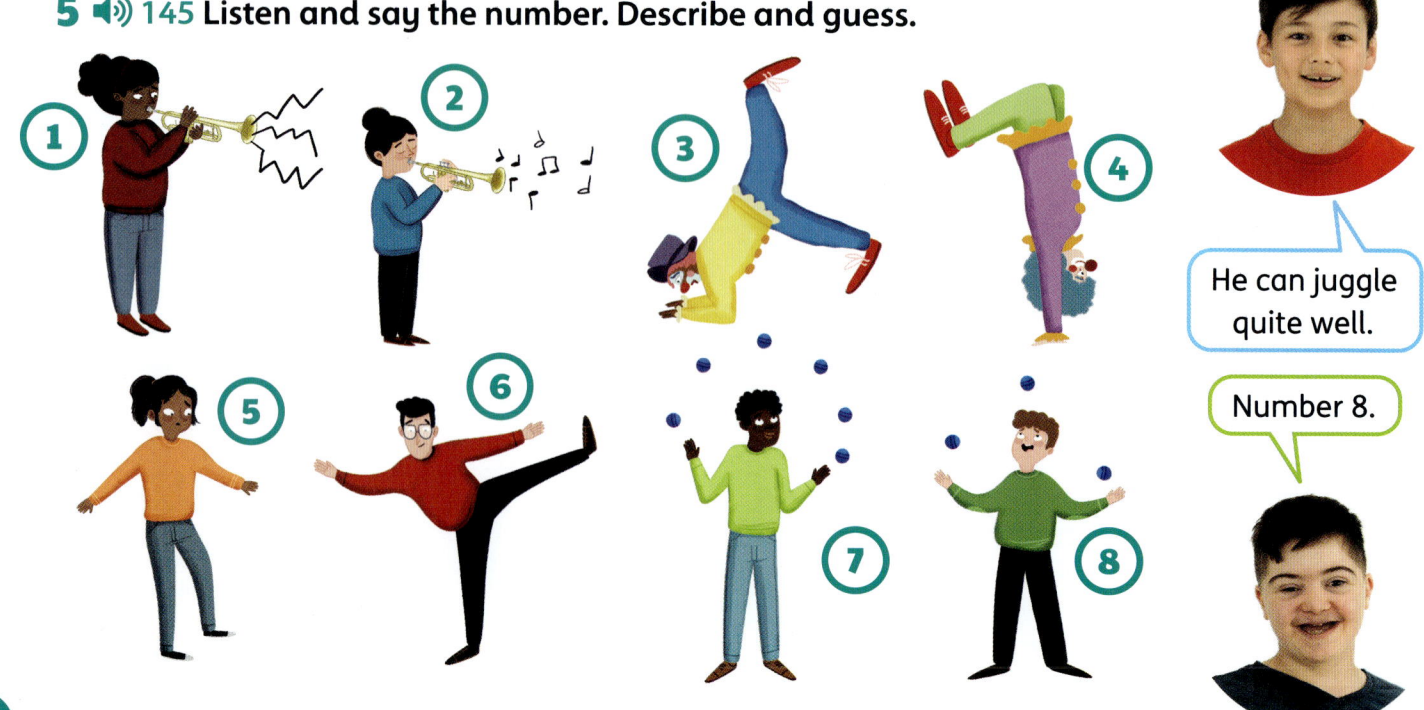

1 2 3 4 5 6 7 8

He can juggle quite well.

Number 8.

64

Listen and speak

Lesson 7 Skills | Unit 6

1 Look and say what you see.

2 🔊 147 Listen and say the number. Listen again. What time is the music show? Write. ✏️

1. Come and see the Amazing Acrobats — 5 o'clock today
2. 
3. 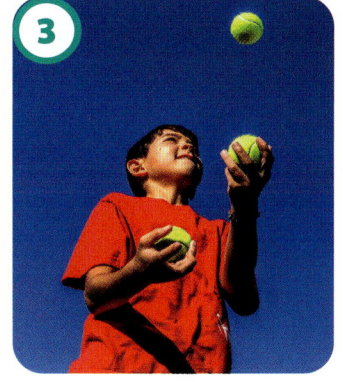
4.

3 🔊 148 Listen and read. Listen and repeat. Act out the dialogue.

— What shall we do?
— Let's go and see the jugglers.
— OK. Good idea. What time are they on?
— Three o'clock. Let's go.

4 **Speak up!** Play the communication game. ✂️ Cut-outs AB page 103

— What shall we do?
— Let's go and see the dancers.
— OK. What time are they on?
— Two o'clock.

Connect — Consider your friend's ideas.

What shall we do?   Let's …   What time are they on?

65

Lesson 8 Review

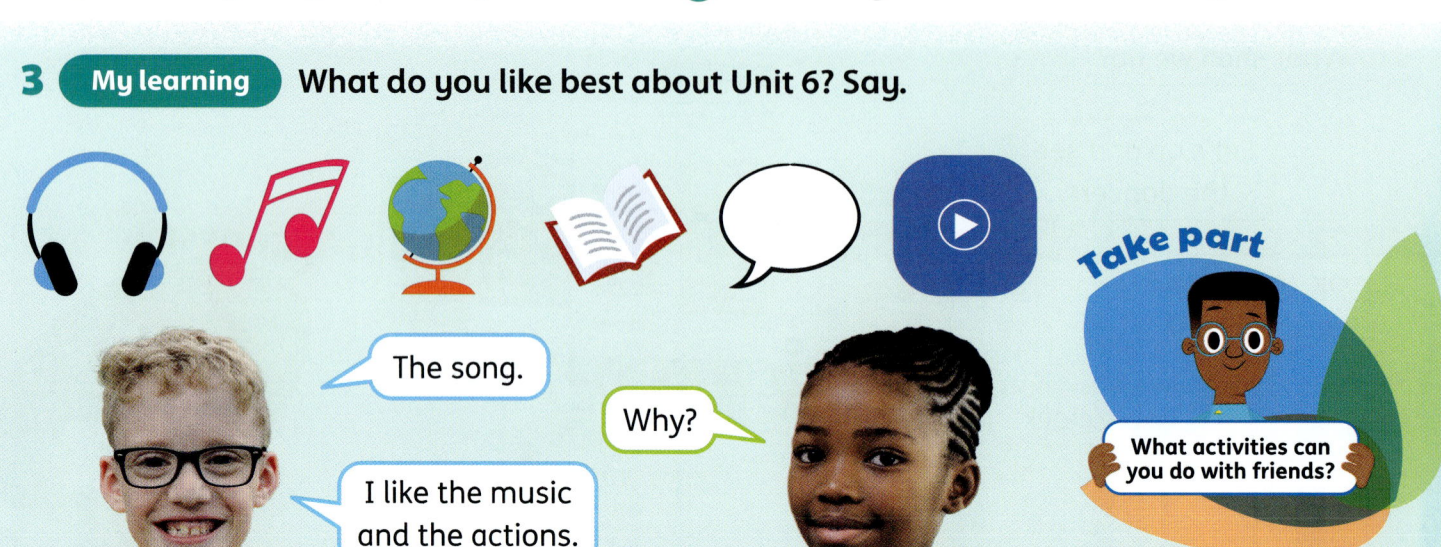

Video

1 👥 Play *Beat the clock* with your class. ⏱

Say 5 skills!

Juggle, …

- 12 — Say 2 things. I can't … very well.
- 11 — Stand still for 10 seconds!
- 10 — Who can do a somersault?
- 9 — Say 4 entertainers.
- 8 — Say 2 things. I can't … very well.
- 7 — Can your friend juggle?
- 6 — Balance on one leg for 10 seconds!
- 5 — Say. I … do a cartwheel …
- 4 — Say 4 things. I can … quite well.
- 3 — Say 4 things. I can … very well.
- 2 — Mime.
  • walk a tightrope
  • play the trumpet
  • play the guitar
- 1 — Remember and say 5 skills.

2 💬 👥 Play the game with your friends. ⏱ Which is your favourite challenge?

3 **My learning** What do you like best about Unit 6? Say.

The song.

Why?

I like the music and the actions.

Take part

What activities can you do with friends?

66

Lesson 9 Project **Unit 6**

Perform a skills show

1 Work in groups. Say.

"What do we need?"

"We need card for a poster, coloured pens, ourselves!"

2 Read and do. **Talk bank**

1. "I can dance quite well." "Great." "Yes!"
Discuss ideas for your show.

2. Collect or make the things you need.

3. Make a poster for the show. Write the time.

4. Practise your skills.

3 **Mediation** Work in groups. Perform the show. Talk about your friends' skills in pairs.

"Welcome to our skills show."

"Sara can play the recorder very well!"

"Javine can juggle quite well."

▶ Video

Channel challenge 3

Video **1** Look and say the words you know.

2 Write a list. Look, cover and say.

animals	bedroom	clothes	activities	food	entertainers

3 🔊 149 Listen, find and say the number.

4 Read and match. Say the letter and the name.

A He's wearing a colourful wig. He can juggle very well.

B He's got a beard. He's wearing a stripy T-shirt. He can't juggle very well.

C She's wearing sparkly sunglasses. She doesn't like lemons.

D She's wearing flowery trousers. She likes grapes. She can balance quite well.

2 Roy
3 Katie
4 Deena
6 Mari
7 Billie

5 Read, find and say. 🔊 150 Listen and check. Write.

1 He's wearing … shoes and a … yellow jumper. He … do a handstand. He's a … .

plain   clown   stripy   can't

2 She's wearing a T-shirt with a … . She … sandwiches. She can do a … very well. She's an … .

likes   cartwheel   acrobat   butterfly

68

Review Units 5–6
Learning situation

1. Grace
5. Benji
8. Orla

6 Do the picture challenge! Say.

Talk bank

I can see some …   I can't see any …

7 Read and do.

Open Up — **Learning situation**

What world festivals do you know about? Create a digital display.

Think I know about …
I want to know about …

Research and prepare

How can you find out about festivals around the world?

□ go online   □ use a library   □ ask a friend

Share your research and create a digital presentation. Use pictures and words!

Present and share

Work together. Give your presentation to the class.

3 She's wearing a … dress and blue … .
She … play the trumpet … . She's a … .

very well   spotty   musician   boots   can

8 Read, think and say.

What's your best work in Units 5 and 6?

What can you improve next year?

Keep learning
Keep practising over the summer holidays!

69

Christmastime

1 🔊 153 Listen, point and repeat.

2 🔊 154 Listen and say the number.

Merry Christmas!

1. sing carols
2. wrap up presents
3. wear Christmas hats
4. make mince pies
5. make decorations
6. put up the Christmas tree

3 🔊 155 Listen, sing and join in.

Christmastime

We're hanging up the stockings.
We're putting up the tree.
We're singing Christmas carols
And making mince pies.

We're wrapping up the presents.
We're wearing Christmas hats.
We're making decorations.
It's Christmastime!

It's Christmastime!
It's Christmastime!
Merry Christmas, everyone!

4 🔊 156 Listen and repeat. Mime, ask and answer.

What am I doing?

You're putting up the Christmas tree.

Easter

1 🔊 157 **Listen, point and repeat.**

2 💿 🔊 158 **Listen and say the number.**

Happy Easter! What do you do at Easter?

1. bake cakes
2. decorate eggs
3. eat hot cross buns
4. give flowers
5. see our family
6. have an Easter egg hunt

3 🔊 159 **Listen, sing and join in.**

Easter song

What do you do at Easter?
Do you eat hot cross buns?
  Yes, we do!
What do we do at Easter?
Do you decorate eggs?
  Yes, we do!

We bake cakes.
We give flowers.
We see our family.

Let's have an Easter egg hunt
And let's have lots of fun.

4 🔊 160 **Listen and repeat. Ask and answer.**

What do you do at Easter?

We have an Easter egg hunt.

71

Friendship Day

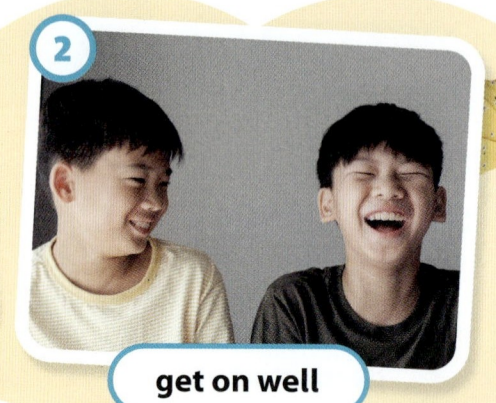

International Friendship Day is on the 30th of July. We celebrate friendship and say *Thank you* to our friends.

1 🔊 161 **Listen, point and repeat.**

2 🔊 162 **Listen and say the number.**

1. send messages
2. get on well
3. make friendship bracelets
4. argue
5. hug our friends
6. give cards

3 🔊 163 **Listen, sing and join in.**

Friendship Day

This is my friend.
She's fun and kind.
She hugs me when I feel sad.
Today, let's make friendship bracelets
And give our friends a card.

Friends don't argue on Friendship Day.
They get on well on Friendship Day.
Let's celebrate our friends today.
Let's get on well on Friendship Day.

This is my friend. She's fun and kind.
She hugs me when I feel sad.
Let's send messages and say thank you
To all our friends on Friendship Day.

4 👥 **Talk about your friends.**

My friend Mo is kind. We get on well. We don't argue.

My friend Yusef sends me funny messages.